A Question of Death & Life

A Catholic Perspective

by
Fr Neil McNicholas

All booklets are published thanks to the
generous support of the members of the
Catholic Truth Society

CATHOLIC TRUTH SOCIETY
PUBLISHERS TO THE HOLY SEE

Contents

All rights reserved. Published 2017. Earlier editions published under the title A Catholic Approach to Dying, *by The Incorporated Catholic Truth Society, 40-46 Harleyford Road, London SE11 5AY Tel: 020 7640 0042 Fax: 020 7640 0046.* © *2017 The Incorporated Catholic Truth Society.*

ISBN 978 1 78469 188 2

An Invitation

As Christians we typically celebrate major life events with sacramental rites and the Catholic Church requires that specific periods of time are spent in preparation for those celebrations. Such programmes can be, as in the case of pre-baptismal instruction for parents, a matter of three or four weekly meetings or, as in the case of ordination, as long as six years – fulltime. However, when it comes to that major life event called death, typically we don't do anything to prepare for it – at least not in a meaningful practical sense, though hopefully the practise of our faith provides a spiritual preparation even though we don't always think about it in those terms.

This booklet invites us to look at our attitudes towards death and to see if we can become a little more comfortable with the prospect of our death as a reality, and then to consider how that might affect, in a positive way, how we live our life – especially as people of faith. And as people of faith – specifically the Catholic faith, we also need to give some thought to practical considerations at the end of life and after death. Again, our ability to do this will depend on how well we have come to terms with the fact that one day we will die.

In terms of my "qualifications" for writing a booklet of this sort, in 1975 I entered the Portland (Oregon) novitiate of the Society of Jesus to begin some eighteen months testing my experience of a vocation to the priesthood. In my second year as a novice, I was sent to the Fred Hutchinson Cancer Research Centre in Seattle – which had pioneered the then very new process of bone marrow transplantation as a treatment for leukaemia – to assist in the area of patient and family support and counselling. By way of preparing for the very real prospect of working with patients and their families for whom the procedure would not be successful, I began looking for books dealing with death, dying, bereavement and grief, only to discover (this was 1976) that very little was available. Thankfully that is no longer the case, but it's still not a subject that people are typically falling over themselves to read about.

Over the years I have given a number of seminars on the subject of death and dying – mostly in parish situations – and that was also the subject of a college course I took, and a component of the university degree that I studied for in the early 1980s. Ironically I had only just completed my degree when I was diagnosed with testicular cancer and found myself contemplating the subject of death from a very different perspective. In 1992 the CTS published the text of my seminars in the first version of this booklet, but this second edition is slightly different incorporating the pastoral experience gained since then. It's also a little more reader-friendly than the seminar presentation.

The original booklet was entitled *Death: A Friendly Companion*, a phrase borrowed from one of Dr Elisabeth Kübler-Ross's books, and after you have finished reading this I hope you will be better able to see and accept death in that light.

The Denial of Death

Let's begin with a story I've come across in more than one source, but here I'll tell it the way it is told in Harriet Sarnoff Schiff's book *The Bereaved Parent*:

There is an old Syrian legend that tells of a beautiful youth, the son of the sultan, who dashed into his father's palace in Damascus crying that he had to leave immediately for Baghdad.

When the sultan asked the lad why he was in such haste the boy replied, "I just saw Death standing in the palace garden, and when he saw me, he stretched out his arms as if to threaten me. I must lose no time in escaping him." Agreeing, the sultan gave the boy his swiftest horse. When he left, the ruler angrily stalked into his garden and demanded to know of Death how he dared to intimidate the son of the sultan.

Death listened, astonished, and answered, "I assure you I did not threaten your son. I only threw up my arms in surprise at seeing him here because I have a rendezvous with him tonight in Baghdad."

The moral of the story is clear – no matter how we may try there is no escaping death. Indeed, from the moment we are born there is nothing more certain than the fact that one day we will die. The question then arises as to why, whether psychologically or emotionally, we try to avoid the reality of death? Putting it more bluntly: why are we afraid to die? Why are we afraid of death?

None of us is immortal

Part of the answer lies in our unconscious expectation of immortality – that part of our psyche that keeps kidding us into believing that we will live for ever. Woody Allen once famously said, "I don't want to achieve immortality through my work… I want to achieve it by not dying!" The fear we experience is a very natural fear of the unknown. If we change jobs, or move house, or emigrate, or marry, there is an understandable tension in leaving behind the familiar, the comfortable, and launching out into the unknown. However, no matter how radical the decision or the commitment, there are all sorts of resources we can turn to and places we can go for advice and help. Even if we decide to go live and work on the other side of the world, we can always go and visit first to see whether we like it or not before we make a final decision.

Not so with death. Death is the ultimate unknown – no one has been there and come back to tell us about it…no one, that is, except Jesus but even what he said, as recorded in Scripture, tends to be expressed through allegory and other literary forms so that we still can't be entirely sure what to expect. All we have are ideas and concepts as in the

Art Garfunkel song "Bright Eyes" (from the soundtrack of the film *Watership Down*). If you can possibly play the song as you read the lyrics you will find that it's a beautiful piece of music to use as a reflection:

Is it a kind of dream, floating out on the tide,
following the river of death downstream...
Oh is it a dream?
There's a fog along the horizon,
a strange glow in the sky,
and nobody seems to know where you go
and what does it mean...
Oh is it a dream?

Bright eyes – burning like fire.
Bright eyes – how can you close and fail?
How can the light that burned so brightly
suddenly burn so pale? Bright eyes.

Is it a kind of shadow, reaching into the night,
wandering over the hills unseen...
Oh is it a dream?
There's a high wind in the trees,
a cold sound in the air,
and nobody ever knows when you go
and where do you start...
Oh into the dark.

Facing up to the fear of death

A man fears death because he fears the unknown. All that man can know is life, and death – it appears to him – is the opposite of life and as such remains dark and impenetrable. And so man shrinks from it in horror as from a fearful and obscene thing. But this is to be oblivious of the fact that Christ has come and said, "I am the Resurrection and the Life." Several other things Christ has said about death are all in terms of life, a terminology we can easily fathom. He has given us to understand that death is not the finish of life. It is the first split second of a new brighter life (*Reflections* by James Turro)

The third century bishop and martyr, St Cyprian, once said in a sermon:

We leave this world in the chains of necessity, rather than in willing obedience. We want to be honoured with the rewards of heaven by the God to whom we come against our will. Why then do we pray and ask that the kingdom of heaven should come, if captivity on earth delights us? Rather let us be ready for all that God's will may bring, with an undivided heart, firm faith and rugged strength. Let us shut out any fear of death, and keep our mind on the immortality that follows death. Let us show that this is what we believe.

Far removed from death

One of the ways in which we tend to deal with our fear of death is by avoiding the subject at all costs. As we'll see, we have turned this avoidance into quite an art. At one time such avoidance wouldn't have been so easy. Infant mortality was high and people died at a much higher rate as a result of poor health care, poor working conditions and the effects of illnesses and diseases for which we now have treatments and cures. When people died, more often than not they died at home and someone in the neighbourhood would come round to lay out the body and prepare it for burial, and the funeral would leave from the house. In many respects death was very much a fact of life whereas nowadays it has become far more institutionalised, and as a result we are more sheltered from the reality of death. Many people now die in hospitals and nursing homes, and the funeral business now provides all the necessary services immediately following death with the body, in most cases, taken to a chapel of rest. I was absolutely amazed to hear a student in one of my university classes in America say that never in her twenty-one years had she been into a cemetery – but that's how removed from death we have become.

Ways we deal with death

To cushion ourselves still further, we have devised an unbelievable number of euphemisms by way of what we might call 'denial vocabulary'. Asked to write down all the words they can think of, people typically manage about ten or twelve (e.g. deceased, departed, passed away, expired). My own efforts produced around fifty! (See the appendix at the back of the booklet.) There can be few, if any, other words in the English language that have provoked such a prolific and creative exercise in avoidance.

One of the strangest ways in which we deal with, or rather don't deal with, the reality of death is by allowing ourselves to be entertained by it – and not just entertained as in sitting and watching but, as in the case of cartoons, laughing uproariously at them and at the horrendous things that happen to the characters. I have to admit that one of my favourites is the Road Runner. How many times in each story do we watch the coyote get flattened by rocks, blown up, knocked down, and go whistling down from cliffs to kick up a tiny cloud of dust on the canyon floor hundreds of feet below? But, of course, no lasting injuries result and no one ever actually dies. We laugh, I'm sure, because the storyline is funny, but also because the characters constantly cheat death and bounce right back again, and that appeals to our sense of immortality.

Whilst our social conscience is beginning to react to the excessive portrayal of violence, death also features quite prominently in many of the films and TV programmes that we watch – not to mention computer games. Why are we comfortable with death in this context? Well, first of all, because most of it is fiction and therefore it isn't really happening, but also perhaps because death usually happens to the "bad guys" – and they deserve it. But let a "good guy" die and that really hits home.

There's also a lot of death on TV news broadcasts, but, because we watch so much make-believe death on TV, it's sometimes difficult to remember that on the news we are watching actual death, and seeing real blood and real dead bodies. It might also seem unreal, or at least non-threatening, because usually it is happening somewhere else to someone else. It's only when horrific things such as accidents, disasters, murders or acts of terrorism happen in our own communities that the reality hits home precisely because it's on our doorstep.

Our relationship with death

Ask yourself: who dies? Our most immediate answers are likely to be "old people", "sick people", "the terminally ill", in other words people we expect to die – and it's generally always *other people*. Did I answer, "I will die"? It's because we're not comfortable with that answer that we react the way we do when, as we've just mentioned, death hits close to home. Death suddenly becomes threatening because whatever the situation, it could just as easily have involved me. Our answer also reflects something we mentioned earlier – our mistaken concept that we are immortal. Even if we manage to think about how things will be after our death, in our mind's eye we're still there, we are a spectator, we are still around.

One of Tom Stoppard's characters gets into a very funny piece of mental rambling on this subject – this is just an excerpt:

> Did you ever think of yourself as actually dead, lying in a box with a lid on it? I mean, you think of it like being alive in a box. You keep forgetting to take into account that you're dead – which should make all the difference shouldn't it? I mean, you'd never know you were in a box, it would be just like being asleep in a box – not that I'd like to sleep in a box mind you, not without any air. You'd wake up dead for a start and then where would you be? (*Rosencrantz & Guildenstern Are Dead*)

Life expectancy versus life expectation

Why can't life be forty or twenty or even ten years? Why do we feel threatened when people die at a younger age? The answer is probably, as we said above, that we expect people to die when they are old and, of course, statistically most people in the western world do reach at least the "three score and ten" of the psalm. However it's precisely that expectation that causes us to react the way we do when a person dies at a much younger age. The lack of quantity (of years) tends to overshadow the aspect of quality (of life) – something we'll return to later. We can't afford to allow ourselves to become complacent and, depending on how old we are, to expect that we'll have a whole lifetime ahead of us. Statistically that might be a possibility, even a probability, but there are no written guarantees and nowhere to ask for our money back if it doesn't happen!

Scripture

You may want to reflect on these passages of Scripture:

John 11:21-27

John 14:1-4

1 Corinthians 15:51-55

1 Thessalonians 4:13-18 (Note that in this passage it doesn't say "don't grieve" but "don't grieve like the other people who have no hope".)

Revelation 21:1-4

Revelation 22:3-5

Death: A Friendly Companion

Who was it who said, "Death is nature's way of telling us to slow down"? A little less dramatically it can at least be a way of telling each of us to take care of a lot of important things while we still can.

It is the denial of death that is partially responsible for people living empty purposeless lives, for if you live as if you'll live for ever, it becomes too easy to postpone the things you know you must do. You live your life in preparation for tomorrow or in remembrance of yesterday, and meanwhile each today is lost. In contrast, when you fully understand that each day you awaken could be the last you have, you take time *that day* to grow, to become more of who you really are.' (*Death: The Final Stage of Growth*, Elisabeth Kübler Ross)

Welcoming the reality of death

The thought that "each day you awaken could be the last you have" could sound very depressing, but it doesn't need to be that way. What it means is that the more comfortable we become with the reality of death, and the less we actually – or at least unthinkingly – deny it, the better and more positively attuned we will be to the day-to-day things that remind us of our mortality. For example, when we hear an ambulance or fire engine siren, does it make us pause and perhaps pray for the person or people in need or do we tune it out because it's something we'd rather not think about? Or what kind of send-off do we give our children and spouses when they, or we, leave home in the morning for school or work? Could we, or they, live with the memory of the last thing that was said or done in the tragic event that it actually was the last thing?

When we stop and think about it, we put a great deal of time and effort (and money) into planning and preparing for all kinds of things that may in fact never happen – career plans, plans for the weekend, planning holidays, etc. As we said earlier, from the time we are born nothing is more certain than the fact that we will die, and yet we generally ignore it and certainly do very little by way of practical (or financial) planning for it. I'm not saying that we should be constantly thinking about death or even expecting death – that would be a morbid obsession – but the fact that without a doubt we will die ought to at least act as a reminder that in various ways, not least spiritually, we should have our house in order.

Kübler-Ross includes an excerpt from a letter written by a physician in which he talks about learning that he had a malignant tumour:

The answer to "How much time do I have?" became "There are x days left, and however long x is there are only two possibilities – to live them in despair, or to really live them to the hilt, making them count." The choice was clear and a great weight was lifted from my shoulders. It would be impossible to exaggerate the significance of that moment. It led to the next realisation that really we're all in the same boat with x days to live. Even if cured of cancer, I'm a day closer to dying today than yesterday. We all are. For all of us then, it isn't the quantity of life but the quality that counts. It took a malignancy to put life into perspective and to open for me the concept of dying as a growing experience.

Consequences of our life and our death

I'm sure you will be quite familiar with Charles Dickens's story *A Christmas Carol*. The visits Scrooge received from the first two spirits enabled him first of all to look back at his life and to see what type of person he had been and then, in looking at the present, to see what affect his life was having on other people. In the third visitation, Scrooge was shown not only the consequences of his life, but also the consequences of his death and it was the sight of his own grave in particular that shocked him into a conversion. He was suddenly faced with the realisation that what he saw of the future, and what he heard people saying about him after his death, were the results of how he had lived his life – and he was far from happy with what he saw. Scrooge was fortunate in being given a chance to see into the future and as a result was able to change his contribution to the present while there was still time and opportunity.

Unlike Scrooge we won't have such an experience, but we can put ourselves in his place and, using a little imagination, try to answer a few very challenging questions: if they spoke the truth, what would people say about you after your death? Would you be entirely happy with what you heard? If you knew you were going to die soon, what difference would it make? Are there things you would do differently? The lesson to be learned, is that if you can see areas for change then why not make those changes now while you still can. I remember in one of the courses on death and dying that I referred to earlier, the lecturer set us the task of doing things the coming week as if we knew we were going to die. Quite apart from having to give a verbal account of what we had done and why, a bigger concern on the day was that ten students were missing!

Have you made your will?

The problem is, of course, that many (perhaps most) people haven't reached the point of being comfortable with the reality of their death and therefore are equally uncomfortable if, for example, someone raises the subject of drawing up a will or asks what sort of funeral they would like. This, they'll say, is being morbid and that they don't want to talk about it – a typical reaction of those in the best of health and the prime of life. People in their elder years are likely to be a little more circumspect and ready to consider and make decisions about these important issues. And that is the point – they *are* important issues and none of us can afford (literally in the case of a will) to ignore them or to keep putting them off.

As surveys show, the majority of people in Britain will not have executed a will. Many people struggle not only to get by financially but to also put a little by for a rainy day and maybe even to accumulate a few creature comforts along the way. How much would we rather see these things passed on to those we choose rather than have them distributed by process of law? – Which is what happens when a person dies without a will. Eighty-two per cent of married people interviewed in one survey thought that, even without a will, their estate would automatically go to their spouse. It won't – not until the courts decide. Surely for the little time and effort that it takes to make a will, and the nominal solicitor's fee involved to have it done properly and legally, it is worth the peace of mind and security of knowing that everything is taken care of.

What about organ donation?

Donor cards, available at most doctors' surgeries, allow you to state which organs may be used for transplantation after your death, and you should then carry your card in your purse or wallet so that it can be quickly and easily found. It's a good idea to make sure family members know that you've done this – better yet, involve them in the process – so that your wishes will be respected and so it doesn't cause even greater upset after your death when those organs are removed.

These are just two practical examples of things that you might want to consider doing, but which you will probably never get round to as long as you are reluctant to contemplate the reality of your death. The point I hope I have made is that such contemplation doesn't need to be morbid, it is merely being realistic. Death is a reality at the end of every life and reaching a point where we can accept death not as a threat, but as a part of life should positively influence so many other things that are equally a part of our life. It's like switching on a light in a room: we don't look at the light, but the fact that it's there enables us to do all sorts of things better than if we were stumbling around in the gloom.

This, then, is the meaning of *Death: the Final Stage of Growth*. All that you are and all that you've done and been is culminated in your death. When you're dying, if you're fortunate enough to have some prior warning, you get your final chance to grow, to become more truly who you really are, to become more fully human. But you don't need to nor should you wait until death is at your doorstep before you start to really live. If you can begin to see death as an invisible, but friendly, companion on your life's journey – gently reminding you not to wait till tomorrow to do what you mean to do – then you can learn to *live* your life rather than simply passing through it. (Foreword, Joseph and Laurie Braga, from *Death: the Final Stage of Growth*)

Implications for our spiritual life

To begin with, our relationship with God probably already puts us in closer touch with the concept of death than might otherwise be the case. Central to our faith is the belief that when we die the quality of our life on earth will greatly influence whether we are judged worthy of eternal life. To the extent that this necessarily makes the mention of death necessary from time to time, it probably mostly happens in church (and we are not always there) and it's something that's going to happen in the future and so we subconsciously file it away under "things to do" because for now we have our lives to live and we fully expect that the future is far away.

When you read the quote from that terminally ill physician who said that whatever time he had left there were two possibilities – to live his days in despair or to really live them to the hilt, I'm sure the words "wine, women and song" crossed your mind – that would be the definition for many people of living life to the hilt. However, what he said was "live them to the hilt, *making them count*" and for us as Christians "making our days count", however many we still have left ahead of us, implies a very different set of values and imperatives.

This is where we owe it to ourselves to turn once again to Scripture. The message is quite clear: don't put off until tomorrow what you mean to do today; don't put off until tomorrow what God asks of you today; don't live today as if there's going to be a tomorrow. In that sense not only is death a friendly companion, so is the word of God, urging us to live each day God gives us in the way we know we should.

Scripture

Luke 12:16-20
Luke 12:35-46 and Matthew 25:1-13
Mark 13:32-37
Wisdom 4:7-15

Talking about Death

Being comfortable with, or at least not threatened by, the reality of death should make it much easier for us to deal with, and respond appropriately to, not only our own experience of death, but also the needs of those approaching death or who have been bereaved.

Speaking with the dying

It is quite understandable, when we may visit someone who is dying, that one of our greatest fears is of not knowing what to say. In a situation like that it is probably better to say nothing – except we are not very comfortable with silence. If a direct question seems inappropriate, one of the best ways of trying to find out what a person's needs are, what's going on with them, how they may be feeling, is to observe and to listen to what *they* tell *us* – trying to pick up on spoken and unspoken clues. But it's very difficult to listen if we keep chatting (and especially about things that are no longer of any interest to the person because of their situation) and they are less likely to be open and forthright if they sense that we are ill at ease. On the other hand, spending time sitting quietly, perhaps holding their hand, lets them know we are there and that we care, and that can be much more supportive. Be comfortable with silence; resist the temptation to fill the time with chatter and distractions, and don't presume the lack of conversation means we should leave. They may need to be left alone to rest – if in doubt ask – but don't use that as an excuse to leave just because sitting quietly, watching the clock, is awkward. One other thing to remember is that if a person is in a coma, don't presume they can't hear what we say. Don't talk about them, talk *to* them and *with* them just in case.

Open communication

As you might imagine, quite unnecessary problems can arise, or can be created, in the area of final health care if there hasn't been honest and open communication – usually because the family has asked that the patient not be told they are dying or, not so commonly, because the patient doesn't want their family to know the seriousness of their situation. In either event the wishes of the patient or family must be respected, but it makes it very difficult for everyone involved. In the more usual former case, not only is the patient being denied their right to know and therefore to be as fully informed and involved as possible in their final care, but also everyone is walking round on eggshells trying to maintain the pretence. If, in fact, the person suspects the seriousness of their situation, they then have to play the same pretending game because everyone else is pretending too. And if they ask the question, it puts their carers in the very difficult position of not being able to answer honestly out of respect for the family's wishes. The situation makes it extremely difficult for the health-care team trapped in that ethical dilemma, and it also denies the patient and their family and friends the opportunity to make the best of whatever precious time may be left.

Speaking with the bereaved

Moving on to consider the situation of visiting someone who has recently been bereaved, if we are unsure about what to say the best advice, once again, may be to say nothing, but rather to sit and to listen. Above all, beware of clichés. There are certain expressions that automatically come to mind in a situation like this but, quite honestly, they are not always as appropriate as we might think and may well sound better in our heads than they do out loud. With the best intentions in the world we can say something which we think is supportive and comforting, but it can come across to the bereaved very differently given the rawness of their emotions at such a time. The sentiments may be admirable, but we just have to be careful about the words we use or the way we say them.

"I know just how you feel." Unless you have been similarly bereaved you don't really know at all, and they may be tempted to tell you so. The question, "How are you doing?" might be a far more compassionate way of indicating that you are concerned about them and it then allows them to answer your question according to how they feel. Nor do they need a 'Job's comforter' retelling your own woes and miseries in a misguided attempt to say you know what they are going through.

"It was God's will." No, it wasn't – death never is and never was God's will (Wisdom 1:13). God doesn't wish grief and sorrow and separation on anyone. Although we think we know what we mean when we say that, it sounds awful and it appears to lay the blame with God at a time when the bereaved person needs to be encouraged to trust in God, a God who loves and cares and will support them.

"He/she is in a better place now." Again we think we know what we are trying to say, but doesn't it sound as if we are saying that being here wasn't as good? We might be able to argue the point theologically, but it's hardly a very comforting or consoling thought and might it not make them feel guilty about wishing the person was still with them, alive and well?

Working through grief

Grief is a very personal and complex emotion, in response to a loss which is absolute and for ever – in this life, at least. It is not only essential, but also literally *vital*, for a person to be allowed to work through and to express their grief. Unfortunately in our society we are uncomfortable with, and often embarrassed by, people whom we feel are "out of control". We tend to be similarly uncomfortable with people crying in public – especially men – and people will even apologise for crying. Certainly in their own homes, or even in ours, people ought to be able to express their feelings to, and in front of, understanding friends. There is even pressure to suppress the emotions of grief: "You must be strong for the children", and a reward system for doing so: "Wasn't it wonderful how strong he/she was?" First of all, it's OK to cry. Secondly grief will be worked out somewhere sometime, and discouraging it at the proper time is like plugging a boiling kettle. When the pressure finally releases itself, as it undoubtedly will, it can be explosive and who knows the damage that has been caused in the meantime.

In the days that follow a death and the time immediately following the funeral, there is usually a constant stream of visitors and friends offering support, cooking meals, and so on. But then it's as if someone dammed the stream and, as everyone necessarily gets on with their own lives, from there being almost too many people around, there may now be almost none. These can be lonely days when the reality and the loss begin to sink in, and it is precisely now that the person may need understanding visitors and support the most.

Visiting the bereaved

This is still a difficult time for visitors – not knowing what to say, feeling particularly solicitous about the bereaved person's feelings, trying to avoid any reference to death or to the person who has died. I've had people tell me that they really wanted, and needed, to talk about them and found it very frustrating when people kept changing, or avoiding, the subject. How do we know, how can we tell? Again – listen and see what they want to talk about, and don't impose your discomfort or unease onto them. It can be very important to the grieving process for the bereaved person to be able to talk to others who are willing to listen and to try to understand what's happening. They need to know that the extreme emotions they are experiencing (being torn inside; afraid that they won't be able to cope; feeling alone and depressed; possibly even imagining that they sometimes see the person who has died) are normal, that they are not going crazy, and that it's all part of the grieving and healing process.

How long will the grief last? There's no easy answer to that. It will come and go – birthdays, anniversaries, Christmas and other holidays will be particularly difficult – much will depend on how well they are working through their grief. It's certainly not right for someone to say, "It's been (such-and-such a length of time) and you should be getting over it by now." How long is "long enough" – six months, a year, two years – who knows? The loss of, for example, a life partner or a child may be an experience from which someone may never fully recover and understandably so. The main concern for family and friends should perhaps be that generally positive progress is being made in the direction of healing, coping and normal functioning. On the other hand it should be fairly obvious when this is not happening and when it might therefore be necessary to think in terms of the need for professional intervention.

Forgotten grievers

It's worth remembering the situation of what we might call the "forgotten grievers" – those not as immediately involved as, for example, a spouse or parent might be. This might include siblings, grandparents, aunts, uncles, cousins, etc. The focus of everyone's concern and support is understandably on the person most immediately bereaved, and others who may feel the loss almost as acutely can be inadvertently excluded from that effort. As a result they have to handle their grief on their own and possibly without others realising their needs. In this regard it is perhaps worth mentioning specifically the problems that can arise in family relationships – and especially within marriages – when individuals either don't share as deeply in a situation of bereavement (for example where a mother may spend a great deal of time with a terminally ill child, but the father has to keep working) or who move through their resulting grief at a different pace or in a different way. This may be another area where close friends can sensitively watch and help.

About unbaptised babies

Traditionally the Church taught that Baptism is essential for salvation, but then the question inevitably arose: what about babies who died before they had been baptised – babies who quite clearly were not responsible for their unbaptised state? The Church had painted itself into a theological corner, and so the concept of "limbo" somehow developed which seemed to satisfy the teaching of the day. It wasn't heaven (for which Baptism was necessary), but at the same time it wasn't hell (a punishment that babies had obviously done nothing to deserve).

In a more enlightened era, post-Vatican II, the Church developed a different understanding. Because a baby isn't capable of committing sin, then why would we believe that its soul wouldn't go to heaven just because no one had yet poured water? In his report of 1985 Cardinal Ratzinger, the future Pope Benedict XVI, reminded us that "limbo" was never a defined truth of faith. The current Catechism simply says of the souls of babies who have died before being baptised that "the Church can only entrust them to the mercy of God" – an affirmation of our faith in a merciful and all-loving God.

Nevertheless it is amazing, nearly fifty years after Vatican II, how many people still seem to be unaware that the Church's thinking and teaching on the subject of "limbo" has changed. As we've said, it isn't even mentioned in the Catechism and yet, rather worryingly, as a concept it is probably better known than many aspects of Church teaching that are!

A Continuum of Care

Particularly for Catholics, there are a number of pastorally important things that we need to bear in mind especially when someone may be dying, but just as importantly – at a time that can also confront us with our mortality – when someone is sick. (And twice there I have used the word "someone", but that "someone" might, of course, be ourselves.)

The revised rites of Anointing and Viaticum – *Pastoral Care of the Sick* – were approved by Pope Paul VI in 1972 and the English translation was published in 1983, replacing the earlier ritual. *The Order of Christian Funerals* was approved by the Bishops' Conference of England and Wales in 1986, was published in 1990, and its use was mandatory from Easter Sunday 1991. These two publications are the foundation of what follows. Together, they provide what might be called a "continuum of pastoral care". Of course someone who might, for example, benefit from the Sacrament of the Sick (which includes the first three of these rites) may not necessarily be dying. Only when death is clearly approaching, or has occurred, would we move on through the continuum.

The rites include:

- Visits to the Sick
- Communion of the Sick
- Anointing of the Sick
- Celebration of Viaticum
- Commendation of the Dying
- Prayers for the Dead
- Vigil for the Deceased
- Reception into Church
- The Funeral Liturgy
- Rite of Committal

The last rites?

It's amazing that nearly a quarter of a century after the revised rites of the Sacrament of the Sick were introduced, people still to this day talk about the "last rites" and their concept is the out-dated image of the priest rushing into the home or hospital, purple stole flying in the wind, having received an emergency call to come and anoint someone who is close to dying or who has, in fact, already died. In an attempt to dispel this image and to give the revised sacrament the place and status it should have, let me quote from the introduction to the "Prayers for the Dead":

> A priest is not to administer the sacraments of penance or anointing. Instead, he should pray for the dead person. It

may be necessary to explain to the family that sacraments are celebrated for the living, not the dead, and that the dead are effectively helped by the prayers of the living.

Please don't put the priest on the spot by asking him to anoint someone after they have died – he isn't allowed to and it's not what the sacrament is for.

Sacraments are for the living

A most important point that may have slipped through the net of catechesis is that sacraments are celebrated with and for the living. Therefore the revised rite of the Sacrament of the Sick makes the point that whenever a person's health is seriously impaired by sickness or old age (or, for example, someone is about to undergo surgery) they should receive the sacrament – which consists of penance (if necessary), Holy Communion and anointing. The whole purpose is to offer the sick person encouragement, hope and strength – and the assurance of the prayer support of their faith community – within the context of a sacramental celebration. And it's a sacrament that can be repeated as often as necessary even within the same situation of ill-health. However, as long as the old image persists then the appearance of a priest at a person's bedside can only bring with it fear and trepidation if they then assume, hopefully wrongly, that they are dying. The Sacrament of the Sick is no longer the "last rites" in that sense.

Viaticum and extreme unction

However if a person *is* dying, hopefully they will already have had the opportunity to celebrate the sacrament in its fullness – in which case the Church has done all it can, spiritually and sacramentally, to prepare them for their final journey. If in fact they haven't had that opportunity, then the priority for the priest is to administer what is called *viaticum* – "food for the journey" – Holy Communion (with penance if necessary and if possible). Receiving Our Lord in Holy Communion is always a priority over anointing. If the person is unable to physically receive the host, either because a 'nil by mouth' regime is in place or because they are unconscious, then the priest will simply anoint them. In such a situation, this is often referred to as *extreme unction* – a "final anointing".

The point to reinforce is that families should be aware of the need to call a priest at as early a stage as possible in the process of a person's illness when the appropriate rite (and hopefully the only rite) they need is the Sacrament of the Sick. If things move beyond that and their condition deteriorates, the person will then have already received in that sacrament – through communion and anointing – all that they need sacramentally. But it should also be remembered that if someone dies without viaticum or without being anointed, family members shouldn't feel guilty about it. God's loving mercy is a far more sure source of hope and comfort than whether a priest was called in time or not – and that's where the "Prayers for the Dead" component of the rite comes in with its message of comfort and hope for the bereaved as well. At the end of the prayers the priest may sign the person's forehead or bless the body with holy water.

Final care

With the continuum of care, we need to mention of the whole area of *final care* – the extent of treatment to be given at the end of life – by way of making the point that this is another important area for discussion with family members. It is also a bit of a 'minefield' – not because the Church's teaching isn't clear on the subject, but because specific decisions require equally specific information from medical staff and much will also depend on the situation to hand. Unless you have a medical background, it is almost impossible to specify precisely what you would want done, or not done, in any given circumstance, especially because a medical intervention that might be merely life-prolonging in one situation could be life-saving in another. For example, you may have said that you never want to be put on a ventilator (thinking in terms of long-term care) yet if you were in an accident, or had a heart attack, the short-term use of a ventilator could be life-saving.

The much misused word *euthanasia* comes from the Greek words *eu* (meaning "well") and *thanatos* (meaning "death") – literally "dying well" and not, as it is often used these days, "being helped to die conveniently". The proper definition is the basis of good and ethical final care in hospital, or in a nursing home or hospice: helping someone to "die well", to be comfortable and free from pain and so to die with dignity and free from distress.

Means to preserve life

A 1996 document from the Bishops' Conference of England and Wales confirmed Church teaching that "ordinary" means of preserving life should be used, but that "extraordinary" means are not demanded. It then continued:

> This is especially true when treatment may be difficult or painful and have no lasting effect. In other words, if a person is clearly soon going to die, medical care may be withdrawn and that person then allowed to die naturally. In a case like this, it is not the carer's intention to cause the death of the patient. In all cases, treatment for pain relief should be given, since this would be classified as "ordinary". Food and water are not medical treatment and withdrawing them from a person is wrong and actually causes death.

The *Catechism of the Catholic Church* states: "Discontinuing medical procedures that are burdensome, dangerous, extraordinary, or disproportionate to the expected outcome can be legitimate; it is the refusal of 'over-zealous' treatment." (2278)

Another source from the United States says:

Allowing nature to take its course does not directly kill the person, even though it may contribute to the person dying earlier than if aggressive treatment had been done. Does this apply to artificially provided nutrition and hydration? When it will allow the person to die from an underlying condition, rather than unnecessarily prolonging their suffering, it may be removed. So, for example, if a terminally ill person's body is no longer able to process food and water, there is no moral obligation to provide nutrition and hydration. However, when withdrawal of nutrition and hydration is intended to kill the person, or will be the immediate and direct cause of doing so, then its withdrawal would be an act of euthanasia and a grave sin against the natural law and the law of God. (*End of Life Decisions*)

Clearly final care is something that you need to reflect on and talk about together as a family, then, in a situation of need, you should be in a much better position to ask the questions of medical staff that you need answering and to make a decision in light of the patient's wishes and of Church teaching. The paragraph from the *Catechism* quoted ends by saying: "The decision should be made by the patient if he is competent and able or, if not, by those legally entitled to act for the patient, whose reasonable will and legitimate interests must always be respected."

Suicide

The death of someone close to us is, for very obvious reasons, a very difficult experience to deal with even if their death was expected. The death of someone who has taken their own life can have an even greater impact for all the same reasons, but also because the bereaved are left with so many unanswered questions and, perhaps, feelings of anger and guilt over what has happened: anger because the act may seem selfish and inconsiderate given the unnecessary suffering it has caused, and guilt over wondering whether something could have been done to stop the person doing what they did. In addition there is also, in people's minds at least, a certain stigma attached to the act of suicide which, for Catholics, results from the Church's attitude in the past towards someone who has taken their own life – I would emphasise "in the past" because thankfully things have changed.

At a time before psychology was even heard of, if someone took their own life it was considered a straightforward act against the fifth commandment – that's how things were understood at the time and so that's what was taught. And because it was considered such a moral evil, someone who took their own life was not allowed a funeral Mass nor could they be buried in consecrated ground. However we are now living in far more enlightened times, the result of due regard being given to the on-going findings of psychology and psychiatry.

The Catechism says: "Suicide contradicts the natural inclination of the human being to preserve and perpetuate his life." (2281) If, therefore, someone takes their own life, it would suggest that their "natural inclination" is not at work. A person can only be guilty of mortal sin if they are fully aware of the seriousness, the moral wrong, of what they are about to do and yet freely decide to go ahead and do it anyway.

More typically a person's decision to end their life isn't that logical. Levels of extreme anguish or fear can build up to a point where those feelings become completely unmanageable and result in psychological disturbance and imbalance. The person isn't thinking clearly; they are lacking judgement; things are out of perspective; life and the threat it appears to hold becomes something they can no longer deal with; ending their life seems to them to be the only way to also end the perceived insurmountable problem(s). Another cause can be what one source calls the "bottomless despair" of clinical depression, the extreme feelings of dejection and hopelessness of someone who feels they are completely worthless and life isn't worth living. Again, the person isn't thinking logically.

Typically there will be a "cry for help" – something, whether in words or actions, designed to alert others to how they feel. The person doesn't really want to end their life, they just want others to know that they *feel like* ending it. Hopefully family, friends or work colleagues will be alert to such a cry. Sometimes, however, it goes unnoticed.

Even given what we have said about how unbalanced a person's judgement is who has decided to end their life, they can be remarkably focussed when it comes to actually carrying it out and very good at hiding their intentions and making everything appear normal. If there are signs, they may be very subtle and easily missed or misinterpreted even by those closest to them. It's sometimes the throwaway remark or the out-of-character mood or behaviour that should alert us, but we understandably resist such thoughts and give people the benefit of the doubt.

There is, I hope, some consolation to be gained by the more enlightened and compassionate pastoral approach that the Church now takes towards the tragedy of suicide. Someone who has taken their own life can now have a funeral service and a cemetery burial the same as anyone else; in fact the *Order of Christian Funerals* even contains a choice of prayers specifically for such a situation – all in all, a complete about-turn from the Church's earlier position.

I like to think that while God was waiting for us to discover psychology and so better understand the mental turmoil that can contribute to a person taking their own life, he was treating such people with the love and compassion and understanding that the Church has now come to accept and teach. Hopefully this might also offer some comfort and consolation to those who may have had family members who committed suicide back in those less enlightened years.

Note: All of this is very different to the situation of someone seeking assisted suicide in a clinic established for that purpose. They have quite deliberately made a decision to end their life – a decision that is planned and premeditated and therefore morally unacceptable, against the fifth commandment, and (for a Catholic) against the moral teaching of the Church. The person who assists them is equally morally guilty.

Funerals: Planning and Structure

Planning a funeral

There are many advantages to pre-planning a funeral, especially because it avoids all the second-guessing, and grief-driven – possibly guilt-driven – decision-making at a time when you are least able to make decisions of any sort let alone about something so important. And following a death you won't have the luxury of time to think things through carefully; decisions will have to be made within hours, or a day or two at the most. Why put that sort of pressure on yourself when you could sit down with your spouse, your parents, etc., and discuss all the options and pros and cons at your leisure, now, when the pressure is off. Ask your priest to be involved and to bring a hymn book round and the lectionary so you can make choices. Ask your funeral director to be involved and to bring his catalogues and the list of his charges. (There may even be the possibility of pre-arranging a funeral, paying for everything ahead of time at today's prices – or at least, perhaps, beginning the process by paying in instalments.)

Get all the information you need so you are happy with the choices you make and the fact of making them together. And, of course, they are not carved in stone (no pun intended) – things can change and so may your plans. In the meantime file the information away somewhere safe so that others know where to find it if and when the need arises.

Who is the funeral for?

There is an important aspect to a funeral that most people probably don't stop to think about, and possibly won't accept at first, and that is that the funeral is for the bereaved, not the deceased. Yes, it is our cultural way of saying our goodbyes to the person who has died and committing their body either to the grave or the crematorium, and yes, it is also the way in which we express our spiritual support for them as we pray for repose of their soul. However the funeral itself – the way in which it is conducted and the elements that are a part of it – is actually for the benefit and support of the bereaved, a first and important step in the process of grieving and healing. That is why, if you ever get round to planning your own funeral, your choices need be made with due regard to how they will affect your grieving family members and friends.

Perhaps the most important of those choices has to do with the form of service that would be most appropriate: a simple funeral service or a requiem Mass. The rite makes it quite clear that the minister "should explain to the family the meaning and significance of each of the funeral rites." This would imply that the family should consider the options in light of pastoral circumstances. (It goes without saying that the Church not only permits, but welcomes the funeral of a non-Catholic spouse or parent but, again, consideration should be given as to whether a service or Mass would be the more appropriate choice.)

Requiem Mass or funeral service?

A basic premise for the celebration of Mass is the full participation of all those present and the reception by as many as possible of the Eucharist which is the fruit of that celebration. If most of the family are non-Catholic or are no longer church-going, then it may not be very helpful to make them sit through the celebration of a Mass they are unfamiliar with or which, ordinarily, they would choose not to attend. It is also questionable to have a communal celebration at which only a handful of people are likely to receive the communal sacrament central to it. To put it another way, if the majority of people are not in communion with the Church, then it is a contradiction for them to have to sit through a celebration that has communion – the Eucharist – at its heart. The same might be said for a situation in which the majority of mourners attending the funeral are not church-going. Mass can be offered for the deceased at any time if that is a concern. The alternative – a funeral service (which includes a Liturgy of the Word but not communion) – may be far more helpful and supportive to the majority of those attending, hopefully leaving them feeling uplifted and consoled by a service that they understood and that didn't rankle with them as an unfamiliar Mass might. Again, Mass can be offered for the deceased at any time.

The General Introduction to the ritual makes this same point when it says: "The Order of Christian Funerals makes provision for the minister, in conjunction with the family, to choose those rites and texts that are most suitable to the situation: those that most closely apply to the needs of the mourners."

It does also say: "When one of its members dies, the Church especially encourages the celebration of the Mass. When Mass cannot be celebrated (i.e. a funeral service) may be used and a Mass for the deceased should be celebrated at a later time."

But one of the reasons it gives to qualify the words "cannot be celebrated" is: "When for pastoral reasons the priest and the family judge that a funeral liturgy outside Mass (i.e. a funeral service) is a more suitable form of celebration."

And what I have said above should be very much a factor in making that decision.

As far as is possible, and allowing of course for the difficult circumstances of bereavement, the family should be involved in planning the funeral – for example choosing hymns and selecting the readings – and also (if commissioned) family members being involved as ministers of the word and ministers of Holy Communion and in any other appropriate aspects of the funeral liturgy.

In terms of the minister who celebrates a funeral: if it's going to be requiem Mass the celebrant will, of course, be a priest, but a funeral service can be celebrated by a deacon (in which case it will be the deacon, not the priest, who will visit the family and make all the arrangements).

The structure of a funeral

The *Order of Christian Funerals* provides for a "Vigil for the Deceased" (which can be celebrated in the home or at the chapel of rest at any time before the funeral) or a "Vigil for the Deceased with Reception at the Church" the evening before the funeral. The practice of the deceased being received into church was almost automatic in certain cultures and communities though it has become less common in more recent times. Like the simple vigil, the vigil with reception involves a short service based around the word of God and prayers for the deceased. It offers an opportunity for friends, neighbours and parishioners to gather in prayer to show their support for the family at a time before the funeral, but it is also an opportunity for those who may be unable to attend the funeral itself to pay their respects and say their farewells.

Arrival and seating

On the day of the funeral, whether it's a service or Mass, when the cortège has arrived and everyone and everything is ready, the priest leads the procession into church, pausing to bless the coffin – the rite suggests at the door, but it can be in the porch (according to the weather) or at the head of the aisle. Usually the funeral director will direct everyone to their seats as the coffin is placed before the altar. (If there has been a vigil reception, and the coffin is already in place, the family will be shown straight to their seats upon arrival.) The convention seems to be for family members and close friends to sit on the left side of the church; only rarely do people seem to spread themselves evenly on both sides. This often means that everyone else tends to sit towards the back unsure of how much space to leave and the right side of the church will be empty, whereas it would be nice if everyone assembled together, as close to the altar as possible, thus also providing a visual prompt to those otherwise isolated at the front who may be unfamiliar with when to sit or stand or kneel.

The options available

A funeral service consists of a Liturgy of the Word (Scripture readings, a brief homily, and prayers of intercession concluding with The Lord's Prayer). There is an option for the reception of communion at this point, but it is rare for a family to ask for it to be included. (If most of the family are practising and therefore regular communicants, they are more likely to have asked for a requiem Mass. I tend to feel that if communion is offered to just a minority of those present – especially a minority of the family – it creates an "us-and-them" situation that I don't think is particularly appropriate.) Next a family member or friend may speak briefly in remembrance of the deceased and then the service concludes with the signs of farewell (the blessing and incensing of the coffin), the prayers of commendation, and the procession out of church to the place of committal.

A requiem is the same as a normal Mass except that the Liturgy of the Word and prayers of the Mass are specific to a funeral. The address, signs of farewell and commendation follow the Liturgy of the Eucharist and replace the normal concluding rite of the Mass.

The service of committal itself is quite brief (being the conclusion of the rite celebrated beforehand in the church) and, whether at the graveside or at the crematorium, should only take about five minutes or so. Mourners may be particularly glad about that if they are gathered at a graveside in the pouring rain or in the depths of winter!

Burial or cremation?

Traditionally Catholics were always buried, indeed cremation was actually forbidden, but for some years now it has been permitted and the choice was up to the person or the family. However in 2016, Rome issued a new instruction regarding burial, and the committal of ashes in the case of cremation.

Rome isn't saying that cremation is wrong and has no doctrinal objections to the practice, but it is now expressing a preference for the burial of a person's body which, as the instruction says, "forms part of their identity – furthermore, burial in a cemetery or another sacred place corresponds to the piety and respect owed to the bodies of the faithful departed who through Baptism have become temples of the Holy Spirit".

In trying to make a choice in light of our belief in the resurrection of the body, people are often concerned about how that will happen and whether burial or cremation will make any difference. The instruction makes it clear that a choice for cremation "does not affect a person's soul, nor does it prevent God from raising up the deceased's body to new life" – meaning that God can raise a body that has decomposed in the ground the same as one that has been cremated, giving us a new glorified body. Exactly how this will happen is a mystery to us, but nothing is impossible to God. "When the last trumpet sounds, the dead will be raised incorruptible, and we shall be changed." (*1 Co* 15:52) "He will form this humbled body of ours anew, moulding it into the image of his glorious body, so effective is his power to make all things obey him." (*Ph* 3:20-21)

If a person's choice, or that of the family, continues to be for cremation, the ashes may no longer be kept in a person's house, nor it is permitted to scatter them whether in the air, on land or at sea, "but (they) must be laid to rest in a cemetery" or "in an area in a church set aside for this purpose". Just as a burial plot provides a physical, on-going, connection with the deceased and encourages us to remember and pray for them, the same is true for the burial of ashes.

A final thought

When someone has died, one of the first contacts you will make will be with the funeral director. It is important to remember (and for them to remember) that while certain practical aspects of the arrangements to be made are their business, certain others are those of the priest. And so, for example, anything to do with the choices and decisions that are to do with the Church's side of things, should not be discussed with the funeral director – even provisionally – until they have been discussed with the priest.

The Funeral: Symbols and Practical Points

Flowers

The instruction says that flowers should be removed from the coffin before it is carried into church – but they may be placed nearby, perhaps in front of the altar to, as it also says, "enhance the setting of the funeral rites".

Candles, incense, holy water

Although the traditional "big six" funeral candles (if churches still have them) may be placed by the coffin, it is recommended that just the Paschal Candle be used as a single symbol of the light of Christ. Blessing the coffin (or, more correctly, the body of the deceased within it) with holy water is a reminder of our Baptism – the sacrament we celebrate at the beginning of our Christian journey. Incensing the body is a sign of honour and respect and an acknowledgement that through Baptism our body became the temple of the Holy Spirit.

Cross

The central Christian symbol of a cross may be placed on the coffin as a reminder that we are marked with the sign of the cross, but most already have a crucifix incorporated into the design.

Bible

A Book of the Gospels or a Bible may also be placed on the coffin as a sign of the importance of the word of God.

Pall

The one remaining symbol, again optional, but hardly ever used, is a pall. This is a large cover that is draped over the coffin as a reminder of our baptismal garment. However they tend to be extremely expensive and are not at all easy to put in place or to remove with anywhere near the dignity required. In addition, I always feel that all they succeed in doing is hiding the coffin from view and in that sense cushioning the reality of the situation, and I don't think that that is particularly helpful. Other non-Christian items such as medals, flags, etc., were not originally permitted. More recently however, it was decided to allow the use of medals and military – but not national – flags because of their connection with the life of the person as commemorated in the funeral.

Liturgical colour

The rite says that "the liturgical colour chosen for funerals should express Christian hope in the light of the paschal mystery, but without being offensive to human grief." Most parishes no longer have black vestments anyway, but the rite suggests that, as a symbolic colour, black isn't really associated with Christian hope. Purple is an option symbolising, as it does, the "expectation of Advent and the Lenten preparation for the paschal mystery." White is suggested as a far better expression of the Easter hope of resurrection just as we wear white vestments at Easter itself. The choice should be made, it says, "in light of local custom…and in consultation with the family."

Readings

The practice has grown up of inviting a family member or a friend of the deceased to read because it seemed a nice thing to do. The problem is that not everyone is used to speaking in public in the way that is required in proclaiming the word of God, and clearly and audibly to everyone in church. And this is important not only because of the specific message of the reading, but also because the readings are the basis of the homily, and if people have had difficulty hearing the readings then the homily may not make any sense either. In recent years the Church has begun to train and commission people to be ministers of the word in order to better assure that the word of God is proclaimed properly and well – and therefore only commissioned ministers should now be asked to read. If a member of the family, or a friend, is a commissioned reader then they may be asked, provided they have had the chance to study and prepare the reading ahead of time. Otherwise one of the parish ministers should be asked or, even though it isn't best practice, the priest or deacon should proclaim both the reading and the Gospel.

Music

One of the most problematic elements of the funeral concerns the choice of music. The rite is very clear on the subject, and it is perhaps worth quoting what it says:

> Music is integral to the funeral rites. It has the power to console and uplift the mourners and to strengthen the unity of the assembly in faith and love. The texts of the songs chosen…should express the paschal mystery of the Lord's suffering, death, and triumph over death and should be related to the readings from Scripture… An organist or other instrumentalist…and, whenever possible, a choir should assist the assembly's full participation in singing the songs, responses and acclamations of these rites.

Subsequent guidelines from the Bishops' Conference have made it clear that, because it quite specifically doesn't "express the paschal mystery" or "relate to the readings from Scripture", secular music is not to be used apart, possibly, from suitably reflective pieces of classical instrumental music and even these would be better played by the organist than from a recorded source. Every parish has hymn books and these provide a more than adequate choice of appropriate hymns, and everyone joining in and singing to the praise of God is infinitely more desirable than sitting listening – even to an appropriate piece of classical music. (Because the committal at the graveside or the crematorium are part of the Church's rites, even though they are not taking place in the church itself, the same guidance on the use of music applies.)

Despite explaining all of this, people (and especially those who are not church-going) often adamantly refuse to accept it, and I have had families insist on pop music being played regardless of what the Church says. A time of bereavement isn't the occasion to get into a discussion like that and, as I said earlier, it would be far better if people would respect the position of the priest in the first place and accept what he is saying as being Church teaching. And, really, that's the bottom line: what we are doing is of the Church and what we do in church should be appropriate to church and to the reality of the presence of Our Lord in the Blessed Sacrament. If people can't accept that and insist on things that are not of the Church, then perhaps they need to celebrate their funeral somewhere else where they can do whatever they like. It's a sad thing to have to say, but it may be the only option if the family creates an impasse like that.

Media presentations

On a related matter, in my own diocese – and perhaps elsewhere too – there is now a policy in place that there should be no use of social media – whether in church, at the crematorium, or the graveside – to record or transmit any part of the funeral service. There are also legal considerations to do with royalties and copyright when music is transmitted and/or recorded in this way. Local funeral directors have been made aware of this policy in case the subject comes up in their initial discussions with families. There also seems to be a recent move towards the use of a PowerPoint-type presentations in place of a eulogy. These are not part of the Church's provisions within the funeral rite anyway (as will be explained in a moment) and would perhaps be far better presented at the reception afterwards.

"Just a few words"

The instructions on the funeral liturgy are a little confusing on the subject of a eulogy. The minister is always expected to give a brief homily based on the readings (with their theme of God's forgiving love and the hope we have in salvation through Our Lord's death and resurrection) but, it says, "there is never to be a eulogy". But then in the rubrics it also says that immediately before the prayers of commendation "a member or a friend of the family may speak in remembrance of the deceased." Isn't that a eulogy?

The problem is that a eulogy, by definition, is backward-looking (looking back over the person's life) whereas the focus of the funeral liturgy is on the future with its message of resurrection and eternal life. The instruction says: "Christians celebrate the funeral rites to offer worship, praise, and thanksgiving to God for the gift of life which has now been returned to God, the author of life and the hope of the just", and I have to say that it always feels strange not making some mention of at least the highlights, a pen-picture, of the person's life – unless, of course, the family doesn't want anything said, or no one feels able to speak.

It should be noted, however, that just as the homily should be brief, so also if a "few words" are to be said about the deceased they should be just that – a few words – and not the long and rambling monologues we often hear. There may well be a time constraint anyway, especially if the entire service is being held at a crematorium where there is usually a strict limit on the time allowed.

There is also a danger of a eulogy painting such a picture of sainthood that, knowing the person as we did, we might begin to wonder if we have come to the wrong funeral! A prominent politician is quoted as saying to the speaker after a funeral: "You never spoke so well of him before" to which he replied, "He was never dead before"!

Children and funerals

The parents of young children are usually the best judges of whether it would be appropriate for them to attend a funeral. If they are going to attend, they should be encouraged beforehand to ask any questions they may have, and these should be answered honestly and openly according to their age. The service in church might possibly be more appropriate than their also going to the graveside or crematorium, but, again, it depends on the individual. Children tend to have far fewer hang-ups than adults do when it comes to dealing with death and, if they have had their questions answered, they may well amaze you with how well, and how frankly, they deal with the whole experience.

*

Part of what I have tried to accomplish by the end of this book is to have helped you to become more comfortable with the reality of death and, in particular *your* death. This then leads on to the realisation that there are some very practical, and at the same time very important, decisions to be made with respect to your death. Just as importantly it has implications for your life. Unlike chickenpox or measles, death isn't "catching" and so there is absolutely no risk involved in thinking about it or even talking about it! But accepting that, like it or not, each of us will die one day and that we can't assume that any one of us is any closer to death than anyone else, we can hopefully see death as a friendly companion. In the words of Psalm 117(118) each day "is the day the Lord has made, let us rejoice and be glad"…today, tomorrow's day, and every day that God entrusts to our stewardship.

Appendix

Dead/Died

Deceased
No longer with us
Slipped away
Left this world (life)
Gone home (west)
Was called
Was taken
Got his wings
In a far better place
Getting his/her reward
Breathed his/her last
At rest (resting)
Lifeless
Lost his/her life
Perished
Kaput
The late
D.O.A.
Pushing up daisies
Met his Waterloo
Bought it (the farm)
Six feet under
It was curtains
Croaked
Popped off
Bit the dust

Departed
Passed away (on)
Crossed over
Went/gone (is gone) (is a gonner)
Gone to his/her reward
Gone to the great (…) in the sky
With the angels
Up there
Met his/her maker
Expired
Asleep (sleeping)
R.I.P.
Free ("Freed from the chains of life")
"Lost" as in "She lost her husband"
It's finished (all over) (ended)
She/he is no more
Didn't make it (pull through)
Joined his/her ancestors
His/her number was up
Cashed in his/her chips
Kicked the bucket (kicked off)
Turned up his/her toes
Snuffed it (life was extinguished)
Checked (pegged) out
Popped his/her clogs

Death

Rest	Loss	Sleep
Departure	Passing (passage)	Demise
It	The end	The Grim Reaper
The grave	Curtains	One way ticket
The other side	Crossing the River Styx	The deep six
Boot Hill	Davy Jones's Locker	The great divide
The great leveller	"Cessation of all vital functions"	

Dying

Fading (failing)	Terminal
Going (Slipping away)	Moribund
Not long for this world	On his/her way out
In extremis	One foot in the grave
The tide of life is ebbing (away)	

20 Answers: End of Life Issues
By Jason Negri

An increasingly contentious issue in the 21st century, questions surrounding the Church's teaching on the sanctity of human life and how it relates to euthanasia and assisted suicide are dealt with in this easily-comprehensible guide. Theoretical and practical issues are discussed and topics covered include legislation on assisted suicide in the UK, Europe and the USA, the importance of palliative care and legal arrangements for those who are dying.

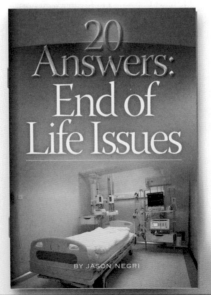

C294   ISBN 978 1 78469 056 4

Living with Illness & Suffering

Nick Donnelly

This booklet of practical advice, discernment and reflection, meditation and prayer has been written for people coming to terms with living with chronic illness and conditions – long-term sickness, disability, grief, depression, anxiety and other forms of suffering. This timely exposition of Catholic understanding of the dignity and value of each life eloquently answers today's vocal minority who press for easy answers including assisted suicide. Accessible and thorough, this text has been written with great compassion and insight.

D727   ISBN 978 1 86082 664 1